HOW TO REDUCE DEFORESTATION BY CREATING AN ARTIFICIAL AND ENVIRONMENTALLY FRIENDLY WOOD REPLACEMENT

How to Reduce Deforestation by Creating an Artificial and Environmentally Friendly Wood Replacement

Walter the Educator

Silent King Books
A WhichHead Entertainment Imprint

Copyright © 2024 by Walter the Educator

All rights reserved. No part of this book may be reproduced in any manner whatsoever without written permission except in the case of brief quotations embodied in critical articles and reviews.

First Printing, 2024

Disclaimer

The author and publisher offer this information without warranties expressed or implied. No matter the grounds, neither the author nor the publisher will be accountable for any losses, injuries, or other damages caused by the reader's use of this book. Your use of this book acknowledges an understanding and acceptance of this disclaimer.

How to Reduce Deforestation by Creating an Artificial and Environmentally Friendly Wood Replacement is a little problem solver book by Walter the Educator that belongs to the Little Problem Solver Books Series.
Collect them all and more books at WaltertheEducator.com

LITTLE PROBLEM
SOLVER BOOKS

INTRO

Deforestation, the large-scale clearing of forests, remains one of the most pressing environmental crises of our time. The loss of forests contributes to climate change, reduces biodiversity, and disrupts ecosystems that are vital to the planet's health. One of the primary drivers of deforestation is the demand for wood. Wood is essential for construction, paper production, furniture, and fuel. In many parts of the world, timber is harvested unsustainably, leading to the destruction of vast forested areas. As global demand for wood continues to rise, finding a solution that can satisfy this need without compromising the environment is crucial. One innovative approach to this challenge is the development of artificial and environmentally friendly wood replacements.

This little book will explore how artificial wood alternatives can help reduce deforestation, examine the properties and applications of these alternatives, discuss the environmental and economic benefits they offer, and propose strategies for their development and widespread adoption.

The Scope of the Deforestation Problem

Deforestation affects tropical rainforests, boreal forests, and temperate woodlands, with alarming consequences. According to the World Resources Institute, global deforestation leads to the loss of around 10 million hectares of forest each year. This has a ripple effect on wildlife, contributing to the extinction of species that rely on forests for survival. Deforestation also disrupts the livelihoods of indigenous communities who depend on forests for food, shelter, and medicine. Furthermore, forests play a vital role in regulating the Earth's climate by absorbing carbon dioxide and releasing oxygen. The reduction of forests accelerates global warming and increases the severity of climate-related phenomena such as droughts, storms, and floods.

The demand for wood products is a major driver of deforestation. Industries such as construction, furniture manufacturing, and paper production consume massive amounts of timber annually. Logging, both legal and illegal, is often carried out in ways that do not allow forests to regenerate. In many cases, forests are cleared to make way for agricultural activities or infrastructure development, but the wood harvested from these lands is often a valuable commodity in itself.

Given the role of wood in various industries and its importance in modern life, it is unrealistic to expect a complete cessation of its use. However, creating alternatives that mimic the desirable properties of wood could significantly reduce the need to cut down trees. By producing materials that are functionally equivalent to or even superior to natural wood, we can alleviate the pressure on forests while meeting global demands.

What Is an Artificial Wood Replacement?

An artificial wood replacement is a synthetic material that replicates the characteristics of natural wood. This material can be used for a variety of applications such as building structures, furniture, flooring, and decorative finishes. Unlike traditional wood substitutes like plastic or metal, which often have a higher environmental cost due to energy-intensive manufacturing processes or poor biodegradability, environmentally friendly wood replacements focus on sustainability from production to disposal.

Modern artificial wood replacements are designed to be strong, lightweight, durable, and aesthetically pleasing. They can be made from recycled materials, biopolymers, or agricultural waste. Some innovations also involve combining different materials to create composite woods, which are engineered to meet specific needs in terms of strength, water resistance, or fire retardancy.

The goal is to provide a sustainable alternative to wood that doesn't compromise on the functionality or aesthetics that make natural timber so valuable. Ideally, artificial wood replacements should be cost-effective to produce, easy to work with, and environmentally benign throughout their lifecycle.

The Types of Artificial Wood Replacements

Several types of artificial wood replacements have been developed, each with unique properties and applications. Some of the most promising options include:

1. **Engineered Wood Composites**: Engineered wood products are made by combining wood fibers or particles with adhesives or resins to create a material that resembles natural wood but with enhanced properties. Common examples include plywood, particleboard, and medium-density fiberboard (MDF). These products are often made using wood waste or fast-growing tree species, reducing the pressure on old-growth forests. However, while they are more efficient than traditional timber, they still rely on wood as a raw material and can involve synthetic adhesives that contribute to environmental pollution.

2. **Bamboo-based Composites**: Bamboo is an incredibly fast-growing plant that can be harvested sustainably. Bamboo-based products, such as flooring, furniture, and construction materials, are increasingly being used as an alternative to wood. Bamboo has excellent mechanical properties, such as strength and flexibility, making it suitable for a wide range of applications. It can also be combined with other materials to create bamboo composites that have the appearance and texture of natural wood.

3. **Bio-based Polymers and Biodegradable Plastics**: Recent advancements in biotechnology have led to the development of bio-based polymers made from renewable resources such as corn, sugarcane, or agricultural waste. These polymers can be used to create wood-like materials that are both biodegradable and non-toxic. For example, polylactic acid (PLA) is a bio-based polymer that can be molded into various forms, including boards and panels that mimic wood. While these materials may not have the exact texture or appearance of wood, they can be engineered for specific uses where aesthetics are less important.

4. **Recycled Plastic Wood**: Recycled plastic wood, also known as plastic lumber, is made from waste plastics such as polyethylene, polypropylene, or polyvinyl chloride (PVC). This material is often used in outdoor applications like decking, fencing, and park benches. Plastic lumber is durable, resistant to moisture, and requires little maintenance, making it an excellent alternative to traditional wood for outdoor settings. However, the challenge with plastic wood is ensuring that the production process is environmentally friendly and that the material is recyclable at the end of its life.

5. **Agricultural Waste Composites**: Agricultural waste products, such as straw, rice husks, or coconut shells, can be used to create composite materials that resemble wood. These materials are often combined with resins or adhesives to create panels, boards, or other building materials. Agricultural waste composites have the advantage of utilizing by-products that would otherwise be discarded, reducing waste and providing a sustainable alternative to wood.

6. **3D-Printed Wood Substitutes**: The advent of 3D printing has opened new possibilities for creating custom-designed wood substitutes. By using bio-based or recycled materials, 3D-printed wood substitutes can be made to exact specifications, reducing material waste and allowing for complex designs that might be difficult to achieve with traditional wood. This technology is still in its early stages, but it holds promise for creating high-quality, environmentally friendly alternatives to wood in a wide range of applications.

Environmental Benefits of Artificial Wood Replacements

The development and use of artificial wood replacements offer several environmental benefits that can help reduce deforestation and mitigate its negative impacts. These benefits include:

1. **Reduction in Tree Harvesting**: The most direct benefit of artificial wood replacements is their ability to reduce the need for tree harvesting. By providing alternatives that mimic the properties of natural wood, we can decrease the demand for timber and slow the rate of deforestation. This allows forests to regenerate and continue providing essential ecosystem services such as carbon sequestration, water filtration, and biodiversity conservation.

2. **Lower Carbon Footprint**: The production of artificial wood replacements can have a lower carbon footprint than the harvesting and processing of natural wood. For example, bamboo grows quickly and absorbs large amounts of carbon dioxide during its growth, making it a carbon-negative material. Similarly, bio-based polymers made from renewable resources can have a lower carbon footprint than conventional plastics or wood products.

By choosing materials with a lower environmental impact, we can reduce the overall carbon emissions associated with construction and manufacturing.

3. **Utilization of Waste Materials**: Many artificial wood replacements are made from recycled or waste materials, such as plastic, agricultural by-products, or wood waste. By using materials that would otherwise be discarded, these alternatives help reduce the amount of waste sent to landfills and decrease the need for virgin resources.

This contributes to a circular economy where materials are reused and repurposed rather than discarded after a single use.

4. **Reduced Habitat Destruction**: Forests are home to countless species of plants and animals, many of which are endangered or threatened by deforestation. By reducing the demand for wood, artificial wood replacements can help protect critical habitats and preserve biodiversity. This is particularly important in tropical rainforests, which are some of the most biodiverse ecosystems on Earth.

5. **Sustainable Land Use**: The development of artificial wood replacements encourages the use of fast-growing and renewable resources such as bamboo or agricultural waste. This promotes more sustainable land-use practices and reduces the pressure on old-growth forests.

In addition, many of these materials can be grown on land that is not suitable for traditional agriculture, providing an additional source of income for farmers without competing with food production.

Economic Benefits of Artificial Wood Replacements

In addition to the environmental benefits, artificial wood replacements offer several economic advantages that can drive their adoption and contribute to sustainable development. These benefits include:

1. **Job Creation in Green Industries**: The production of artificial wood replacements creates new opportunities for employment in industries focused on sustainable materials and technologies.

From the cultivation of renewable resources like bamboo to the manufacturing of bio-based polymers and recycled materials, these industries have the potential to provide green jobs that support environmental goals. This can be particularly beneficial in regions where deforestation has led to job losses in traditional logging or farming industries.

2. **Cost-Effectiveness**: As technology advances and production scales up, artificial wood replacements are becoming more cost-effective. In some cases, they may be cheaper than natural wood, particularly when considering the long-term costs associated with wood maintenance, such as treatments for rot, pests, or weathering. For example, plastic lumber and bamboo-based products often require less maintenance and have longer lifespans than traditional wood, making them a more economical choice for outdoor applications.

3. **Energy Efficiency in Production**: Some artificial wood replacements, such as bamboo composites or biopolymers, require less energy to produce than traditional wood or other building materials like steel or concrete. This can lead to cost savings in terms of energy consumption and reduce the overall environmental impact of the production process. As energy prices continue to rise, materials that are more energy-efficient to produce will become increasingly attractive to manufacturers and consumers alike.

4. **Reduced Transportation Costs**: Because artificial wood replacements can often be produced locally from renewable or recycled materials, they may help reduce the need for long-distance transportation of timber. This can lower transportation costs and decrease the carbon emissions associated with shipping wood products from forested regions to manufacturing or construction sites.

5. **Innovation and Competitive Advantage**: Companies that invest in the development and production of artificial wood replacements may gain a competitive advantage in the market. As consumers become more environmentally conscious, there is growing demand for sustainable products that have minimal impact on the planet.

By offering eco-friendly alternatives to wood, companies can differentiate themselves from competitors and attract environmentally minded consumers.

Challenges and Opportunities for Adoption

Despite the many benefits of artificial wood replacements, several challenges must be addressed to ensure their widespread adoption. These challenges include:

1. **Consumer Perception and Preferences**: Many consumers are accustomed to the look and feel of natural wood, and may be hesitant to adopt artificial wood replacements. To overcome this, it is important to raise awareness about the environmental benefits of these alternatives and highlight their advantages in terms of durability, cost, and performance. In addition, manufacturers should focus on developing artificial wood replacements that closely mimic the aesthetic qualities of natural wood.

2. **Material Performance and Quality**: While some artificial wood replacements, such as engineered wood composites and bamboo-based products, have proven to be highly durable and reliable, others may still face challenges in terms of performance. For example, some bio-based polymers may not have the same strength or water resistance as natural wood. Continued research and development are needed to improve the quality and performance of artificial wood replacements and ensure that they meet the needs of various industries.

3. **Regulatory and Policy Support**: Governments and policymakers play a crucial role in promoting the adoption of artificial wood replacements. This can be done by offering incentives for companies that develop and use sustainable materials, implementing regulations that encourage the use of eco-friendly alternatives, and supporting research and development in this field. Public procurement policies that prioritize sustainable materials in construction projects can also help drive demand for artificial wood replacements.

4. **Infrastructure and Supply Chains**: The production of artificial wood replacements requires specialized infrastructure and supply chains, particularly for materials like biopolymers or bamboo composites. In some regions, the lack of access to these materials or technologies may hinder their adoption. To address this, investments in infrastructure and capacity-building are needed to ensure that artificial wood replacements are widely available and affordable.

Conclusion

Reducing deforestation is a critical challenge that requires innovative solutions to meet the global demand for wood while protecting the environment. Artificial wood replacements offer a promising path forward by providing sustainable alternatives to natural timber. These materials can reduce the need for tree harvesting, lower carbon emissions, and promote the use of renewable and recycled resources. By addressing the challenges of consumer perception, material performance, and infrastructure, we can accelerate the adoption of artificial wood replacements and make significant progress in the fight against deforestation.

In the coming decades, the development and use of environmentally friendly wood replacements will play an increasingly important role in sustainable construction, manufacturing, and design. By embracing these innovations, we can help protect the world's forests, preserve biodiversity, and create a more sustainable future for all.

ABOUT THE CREATOR

Walter the Educator is one of the pseudonyms for Walter Anderson. Formally educated in Chemistry, Business, and Education, he is an educator, an author, a diverse entrepreneur, and he is the son of a disabled war veteran. "Walter the Educator" shares his time between educating and creating. He holds interests and owns several creative projects that entertain, enlighten, enhance, and educate, hoping to inspire and motivate you. Follow, find new works, and stay up to date with Walter the Educator™ at WaltertheEducator.com

www.ingramcontent.com/pod-product-compliance
Lightning Source LLC
LaVergne TN
LVHW051922060526
838201LV00060B/4132